PIANO | VOCAL | GUITAR

TOP COUNTRY HITS OF '00-'01

ISBN 0-634-02973-8

7777 W. BLUEMOUND RD. P.O. BOX 13819 MILWAUKEE, WI 53213

For all works contained herein:
Unauthorized copying, arranging, adapting, recording or public performance is an infringement of copyright.
Infringers are liable under the law.

Visit Hal Leonard Online at
www.halleonard.com

CONTENTS

3	AMAZED	Lonestar
8	BEST OF INTENTIONS	Travis Tritt
14	BORN TO FLY	Sara Evans
22	BREATHE	Faith Hill
28	BURN	Jo Dee Messina
34	BUY ME A ROSE	Kenny Rogers with Alison Krauss & Billy Dean
40	COWBOY TAKE ME AWAY	Dixie Chicks
48	I HOPE YOU DANCE	Lee Ann Womack with Sons of the Desert
56	I NEED YOU	LeAnn Rimes
64	I WILL...BUT	SHeDAISY
70	JUST ANOTHER DAY IN PARADISE	Phil Vassar
84	KISS THIS	Aaron Tippin
77	LET'S MAKE LOVE	Faith Hill with Tim McGraw
90	A LITTLE GASOLINE	Terri Clark
96	LOVE'S THE ONLY HOUSE	Martina McBride
112	MY BEST FRIEND	Tim McGraw
118	MY NEXT THIRTY YEARS	Tim McGraw
126	ONE VOICE	Billy Gilman
130	THE WAY YOU LOVE ME	Faith Hill
107	WE DANCED	Brad Paisley
138	WHAT ABOUT NOW	Lonestar
134	WITHOUT YOU	Dixie Chicks

AMAZED

Words and Music by MARV GREEN, CHRIS LINDSEY and AIMEE MAYO

Ev-'ry time our eyes meet, this feel-in' in-side me is al-most more than I can take.
The smell of your skin, the taste of your kiss, the way you whis-per in the dark.

*Recorded a half step lower.

Copyright © 1998 by Careers-BMG Music Publishing, Inc., Silverkiss Music Publishing,
Songs Of Nashville DreamWorks, Warner-Tamerlane Publishing Corp. and Golden Wheat Music
All Rights for Silverkiss Music Publishing Administered by Careers-BMG Music Publishing, Inc.
All Rights for Songs Of Nashville DreamWorks Administered by Cherry River Music Co.
All Rights for Golden Wheat Music Administered by Warner-Tamerlane Publishing Corp.
International Copyright Secured   All Rights Reserved

BEST OF INTENTIONS

Words and Music by
TRAVIS TRITT

Copyright © 2000 Post Oak Publishing, Inc.
International Copyright Secured   All Rights Reserved

BREATHE

Words and Music by HOLLY LAMAR
and STEPHANIE BENTLEY

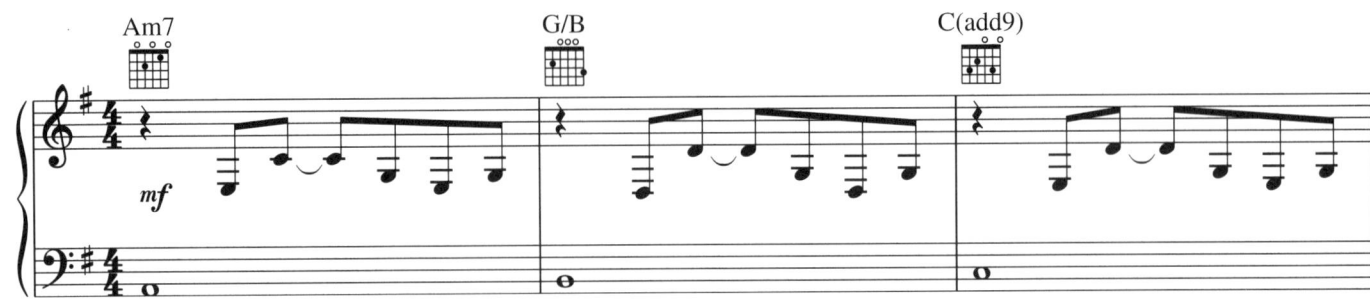
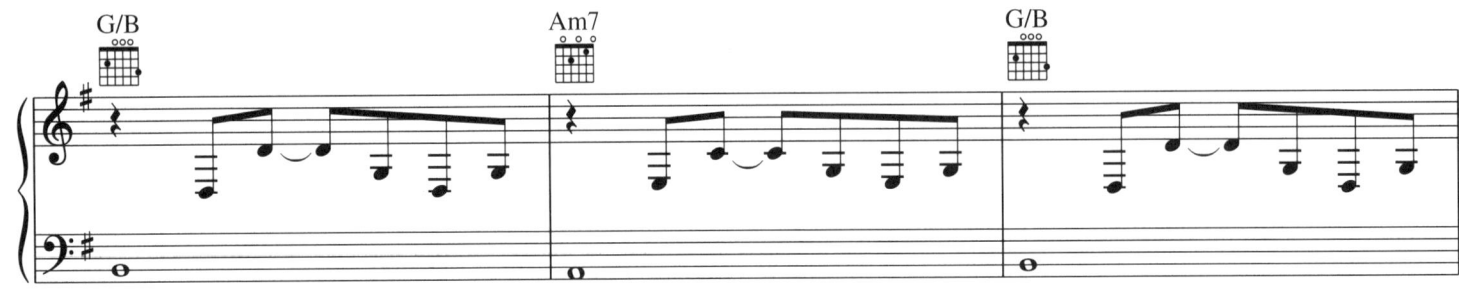

Copyright © 1999 Cal IV Songs, Universal - Songs Of PolyGram International, Inc. and Hopechest Music
All Rights on behalf of Cal IV Songs Administered by Cal IV Entertainment, Inc., 808 19th Avenue South, Nashville, TN 37203
All Rights Reserved   Used by Permission

BUY ME A ROSE

Words and Music by ERIK HICKENLOOPER and JIM FUNK

more that he lives ____ the less that he tries ____ to show her the love ____ that he holds in-side. ____ And the more that she gives ____ the more that he sees ____ this is a sto-ry of you ____ and me. ____ *Both:* So, I bought you a rose ____

E♭
Cm7
A♭6
on the way home from work
to o - pen the door to a heart that I hurt.
B♭7
E♭/G
And I hope you no - ticed this look in my eyes
A♭
E♭/G
(Male:) 'cause I'm gon - na make things right
B♭
E♭
for the rest of your life.

Cm
3 fr
B♭
A♭
4 fr
Both: And I'm gon - na hold you to - night,
E♭/G
3 fr
B♭
(Male:) do all those lit - tle things for the rest of your life.
E♭
3 fr
A♭
4 fr
A♭/C
3 fr
B♭7
E♭(add2)
rit.

COWBOY TAKE ME AWAY

Words and Music by MARTIE SEIDEL and MARCUS HUMMON

Original key: F# major. This edition has been transposed up one half-step to be more playable.

© 1999 WOOLLY PUDDIN' MUSIC (BMI)/Administered by BUG MUSIC, CAREERS-BMG MUSIC PUBLISHING, INC. and FLOYD'S DREAM MUSIC
All Rights for FLOYD'S DREAM MUSIC Administered by CAREERS-BMG MUSIC PUBLISHING, INC.
All Rights Reserved   Used by Permission

grow some-thing wild and un-rul-y. I wan-na sleep on the hard ground in the com-fort of your arms on a pil-low of blue bon-nets and a blan-ket made of stars. Oh, it sounds good to me. I said, cow-boy,

G G/B Am7 D/B D
7 fr
take me a - way. Fly this girl as high
Em C D
as you can in - to the wild blue. Set me
G G/B Am7 D/B D
7 fr
free, oh, I pray, clos - er to
Em C D
heav-en a - bove and clos - er to you, clos - er to you.

Lyrics:

I wan-na walk and not run. ___ I wan-na skip and not ___ fall. ___ I wan-na look at the ___ ho-ri-zon and not see ___ a build-ing stand-in' tall. ___ I wan-na be the on-ly one ___ for miles and miles _____ ex - cept for may - be you __ and your

sim-ple smile. __ Oh, it sounds good to me. __ Yes, it sounds __

__ so good __ to me. __ Cow-boy, take __ me __ a - way.

Fly this girl __ as high __ as you can __ in - to the wild __ blue. __

Set me free, oh, I pray, closer to heaven above and closer to you, closer to you.

I said_ I wan-na touch the earth,_ I wan-na break it in_ my hands._ I wan-na grow some-thing wild_ and un-rul-y._ Oh, it sounds_

D.S. al Coda

47

Clos - er to you.

Cow - boy, take me a - way, clos - er to you.

Instrumental ad lib.

I HOPE YOU DANCE

Words and Music by TIA SILLERS
and MARK D. SANDERS

Moderately

hope you nev-er lose _____ your sense of won-der.
nev-er fear _____ those _____ moun-tains in the dis-tance.

Copyright © 2000 by Choice Is Tragic Music, Ensign Music Corporation, Soda Creek and Universal - MCA Music Publishing,
A Division Of Universal Studios, Inc.
International Copyright Secured   All Rights Reserved

You get your fill to eat, but always keep that hunger. May you never take one single breath for granted. God forbid love ever leave you empty handed.

Never settle for the path of least resistence. Livin' might mean takin' chances if they're worth takin'. Lovin' might be a mistake, but it's worth makin'.

I hope you still feel small when you stand be-side the o-cean. When-ev-er one door clos-es, I hope one more o-pens. Prom-ise me that you'll give faith a fight-ing

Don't let some hell-bent heart leave you bit-ter. When you come close to sell-in' out, re-con-sid-er. Give the heav-ens a-bove more than just a pass-ing

chance.
glance. And when you get the choice to

sit it out or dance, I hope you dance.

I hope you dance.

Fsus F
2 Gm Eb
Time is a
I hope you
Bb F/A
wheel in con - stant mo - tion, al - ways roll -
I hope you
Gm Eb
- ing us a - long.
dance.
Fsus F Gm Eb
Tell me, who wants to
I hope you dance.

B♭
F/A
look back on their youth and won - der where
I hope you
Gm
3 fr
E♭
3 fr
Fsus
F
those years have gone?
dance.
D.S. al Coda
I hope you still
CODA
Fsus
N.C.
dance.
Gm
3 fr
E♭
3 fr
B♭
F/A
Dance,

Gm
3 fr
Eb
3 fr
I hope you dance.
Fsus
F
Gm
3 fr
Eb
3 fr
Time is a
I hope you dance.
Bb
F/A
wheel in con - stant mo - tion, al - ways roll -
I hope you
Gm
3 fr
Eb
3 fr
- ing us a - long.
dance.

Fsus
F
Gm
3 fr
Eb
3 fr
Tell me, who wants to
I hope you dance.
Bb
F/A
look back on their youth and won - der where
I hope you
Repeat and Fade
Gm
3 fr
Eb
3 fr
Fsus
F
those years have gone?
dance.
Optional Ending
Fsus
F
Bb
I hope you dance.
rit.

I NEED YOU
featured in the Epic Mini-Series JESUS

Words and Music by DENNIS MATKOSKY
and TY LACY

Moderately in 2

*Vocal line written one octave higher than sung.

I don't need a lot ____ of things; I can

© 2000 EMI APRIL MUSIC INC., JESKAR MUSIC and ARIOSE MUSIC
All Rights for JESKAR MUSIC Controlled and Administered by EMI APRIL MUSIC INC.
All Rights for ARIOSE MUSIC Controlled and Administered by EMI CHRISTIAN MUSIC PUBLISHING
All Rights Reserved   International Copyright Secured   Used by Permission

Em9
Cmaj9
G
get by with noth - ing. Of all the bless - ings life
can bring, I've al - ways need - ed some - thing.
Em9
Cmaj9
Am11
5 fr
G/B
But I've got all I want when it comes to lov - ing You.
Am11
5 fr
You're my on - ly rea - son,

C(add9)
D
G
D/F♯
You're my on - ly truth. I need You like wa -
D
C(add2)
Am11
5 fr
- ter, like breath, like rain. I need You
Em11
7 fr
Bm7
2 fr
C(add2)
like mer - cy from heav - en's gate.
Am11
5 fr
G/B
There's a free - dom in Your arms that

car - ries me through. I need You.

You're the hope that moves me to

courage a-gain, _____ oh, yeah. _____ You're the love that res-

-cues me when the cold _____ winds rage. _____

And it's so a-maz-ing, 'cause that's just how You are. _____

And I can't turn back _____ now, 'cause You've

brought me too far. _____ I ____ need You ____

CODA

Oh ____ yes, I ____ do, ____

____ oh. ____ I need you ____

like wa-ter, like breath, like rain. I need You like mer-cy from heav-en's gate. There's a free-dom in Your arms that car-ries me through. I need You,

63

Lead vocal ad lib. 2nd time

oh, yes I do.

Repeat and Fade

I need You.

Optional Ending

rit.

I WILL...BUT

Words and Music by KRISTYN OSBORN
and JASON DEERE

Moderately bright

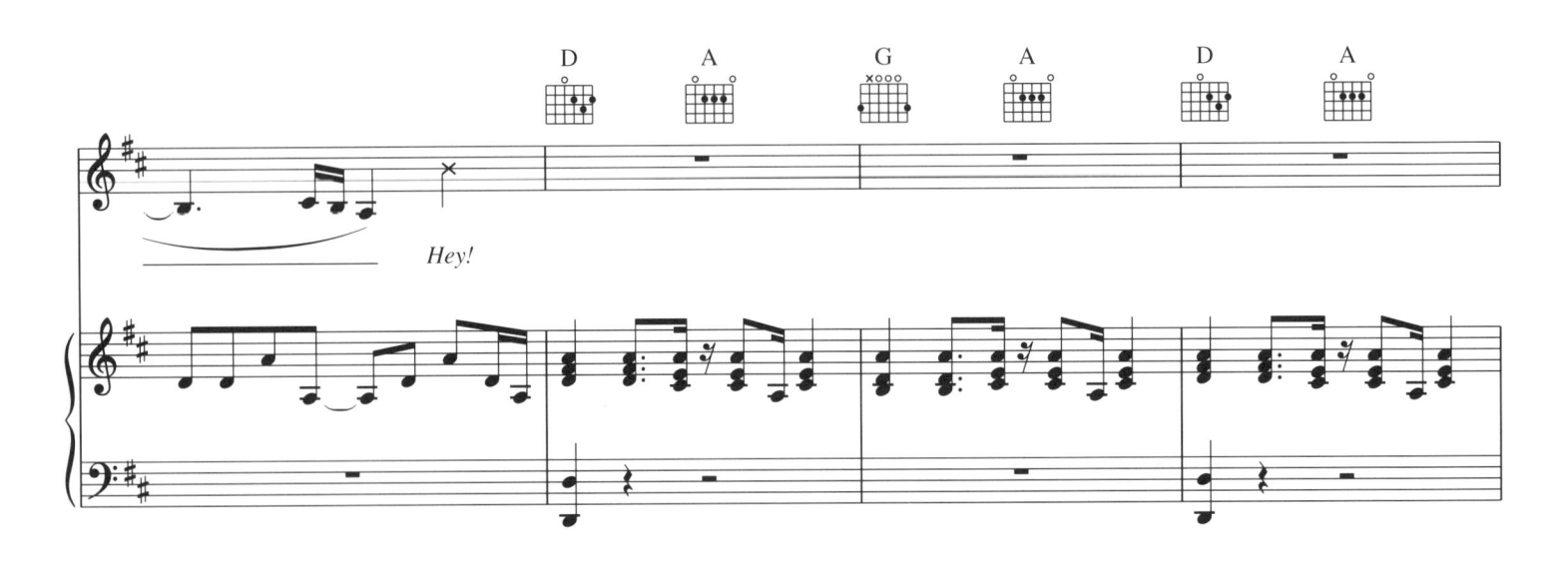

I won't be bored; I won't be ignored. Hey!

I won't be your dirty secret.
I won't be your crutch to lean on.

Copyright © 1999 Without Anna Music (ASCAP) and Lehsem Music, LLC (ASCAP)
Lehsem Music, LLC Administered by Music & Media International, Inc.
International Copyright Secured All Rights Reserved

65

I won't be your cure-all pill. And I won't run to fetch the water just to tumble down the hill.
I won't wear stiletto heels. I won't walk a mile in your shoes just so I know how it feels.

I won't be your Friday paycheck. I won't be the prize you flaunt.
I won't be your obligation. I won't be your Barbie doll.

And I won't be your Martha Stewart, baby,
I won't be the portrait of perfec-

or your all-night restaurant.
tion to adorn your wall. } But I will,

I will, I will be your everything (if you make me feel
like a woman should.) I will, I will, I will be the whole shebang.

You know I will. But But

hey, _____ you know, you know _ I will, all right.

I won't _ be your life-time girl-friend. _

I won't _ be just one of the guys. _ I won't _ be your ma-

D.S. al Coda

ma's fa-v'rite. I re-fuse to be the last in ___ line. ___ But I will,

Coda

___ Yeah, I will, I will, I will ___ be your ev - er - y - thing. ___

___ I will, I will ___ be the whole ___ she - bang. ___ I will, I will ___

___ be your ev - er - y - thing. ___ I will, I will, I will, I ___

will, _____ yeah. _____ You know I will, _ you

know, you know I will. _____ You know I will, _ you

know, you know I will, _____ yeah. _____

JUST ANOTHER DAY IN PARADISE

Words and Music by PHIL VASSAR
and CRAIG WISEMAN

stack of bills, over-due. Good mornin', baby,
res-tau-rant. You start to cry. Baby, we'll just

how are you? Got-ta half hour, a quick show-er.
im-pro-vise. Well, Plan B, looks like

Take a drink of milk, but the milk's gone sour. My fun-ny face
Dom-i-no's Piz-za in the can-dle light. Then we'll tip-py toe

makes you laugh. Twist the top on and I put it back.
to our room and make a lit-tle love that's o-ver-due. But

| Bm | A | G |

There goes the wash-in' ma-chine.
some-bod-y had a bad dream.

| A Bm | A |

Ba - by, don't kick it, prom - ise I'll fix it
Ma - ma, and dad - dy, can me and my ted - dy

| Em7 D/F# | G A | D |

long with 'bout a mil - lion oth - er things. Well it's
come in and sleep in be - tween. Yeah, it's

O K, it's

| G | A | D |

so nice. It's just an - oth - er day in par - a - dise. Well there's no place that I'd rather be.

Well it's two hearts and one dream.

I wouldn't trade it for anything. And I ask the Lord

ev-'ry night, ooh, for just an-oth-er day in

1
D
D/F♯
G
par - a - dise.
Bm
A
N.C.
2
D
D/F♯
par - a - dise.
G
Bm
A
D
Whoa, well it's O K, it's
G
A
D
D.S. al Coda
so nice, just an - oth - er day in par - a - dise. Well there's

par - a - dise.

Just an-oth-er day in par-a-dise. _____

Well it's the kids scream-in', the phone ring-in', just an-oth-er day. _____ Well,

D
D/F♯
G
Fri - day,
you're late,
Bm
A
D
D/F♯
oh.
G
A
D
It's just an - oth - er day in par - a - dise.
D/F♯
G
Bm
A
D

LET'S MAKE LOVE

*Words and Music by BILL LUTHER, AIMEE MAYO,
CHRIS LINDSEY and MARV GREEN*

(Female:) Baby, I've been drifting away, dreaming all day of holding you, touching you.

Copyright © 1999 by Careers-BMG Music Publishing, Inc., Songs Of Nashville DreamWorks,
Warner-Tamerlane Publishing Corp. and Golden Wheat Music
All Rights for Songs Of Nashville DreamWorks Administered by Cherry River Music Co.
All Rights for Golden Wheat Music Administered by Warner-Tamerlane Publishing Corp.
International Copyright Secured   All Rights Reserved

Lyrics:
The only thing I wanna do is be with you, as close to you as I can be. And let's make love all night long until all our strength is gone.

E♭
B♭
And hold on tight, just let
F
Gm
go. I wan - na feel you in my soul.
E♭
Cm7
B♭/D
E♭
F
Un - til the sun comes up, let's make
B♭
F/A
Gm
B♭/F
love.

(Male:) Do you know what you do to me? Ev-'ry-thing in-side of me is want-ing you and need-ing you. I'm so in love with you.

Look in my eyes, ___ let's get lost to-night ___ in each oth - er. Both: Let's make love all night __ long un - til all our __ strength __ is gone. __ Hold on ___ tight, just let ___

D
Em
C
To Coda
(Male:)
go. I wan-na feel you in my soul. Un -
Am7
G/B
C
D
Both:
G
F/A
til the sun comes up, let's make love.
B♭
F/A
Gm
3 fr
B♭/F
Dsus
N.C.
D.S. al Coda
Let's make

CODA
Am7
G/B
C
(Female:) Oh,
til the sun comes up,
(Female:) un -
Am7
G/B
Csus2
Dsus
til the sun comes up,
Both: let's make
G
D/F♯
love.
3
Em
Csus2
G
(Male:) all night long,
(Female:) Let's make love all night long. Let's make love.
rit.

KISS THIS

Words and Music by AARON TIPPIN, THEA TIPPIN and PHILLIP DOUGLAS

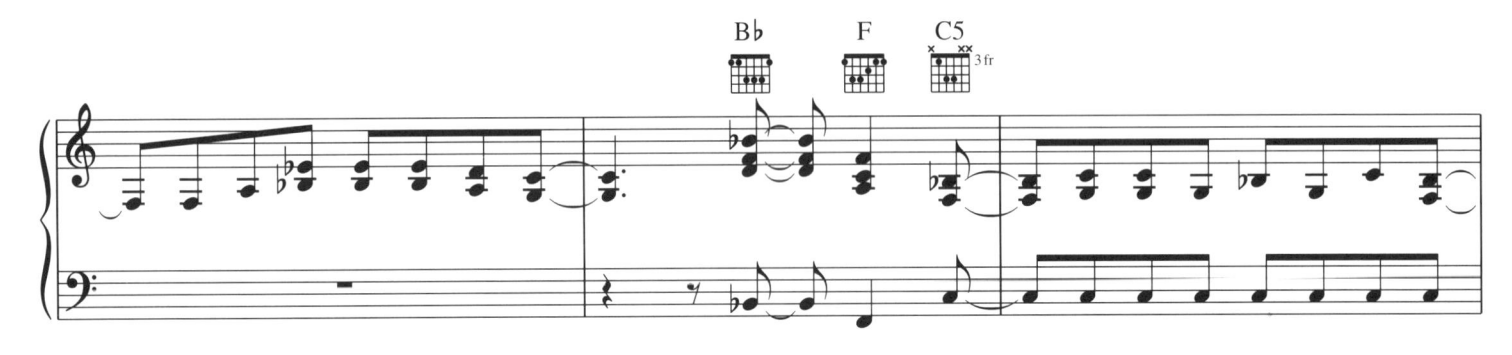

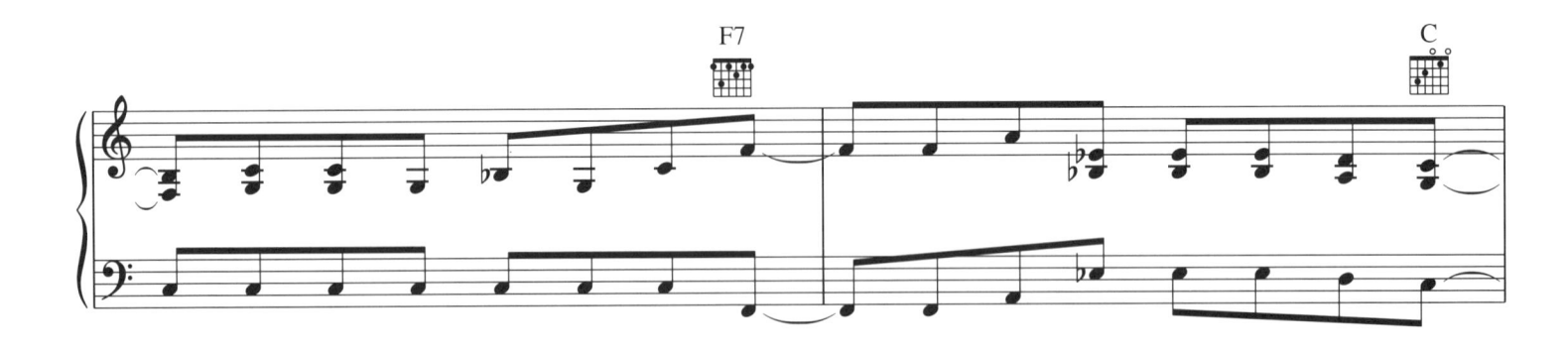

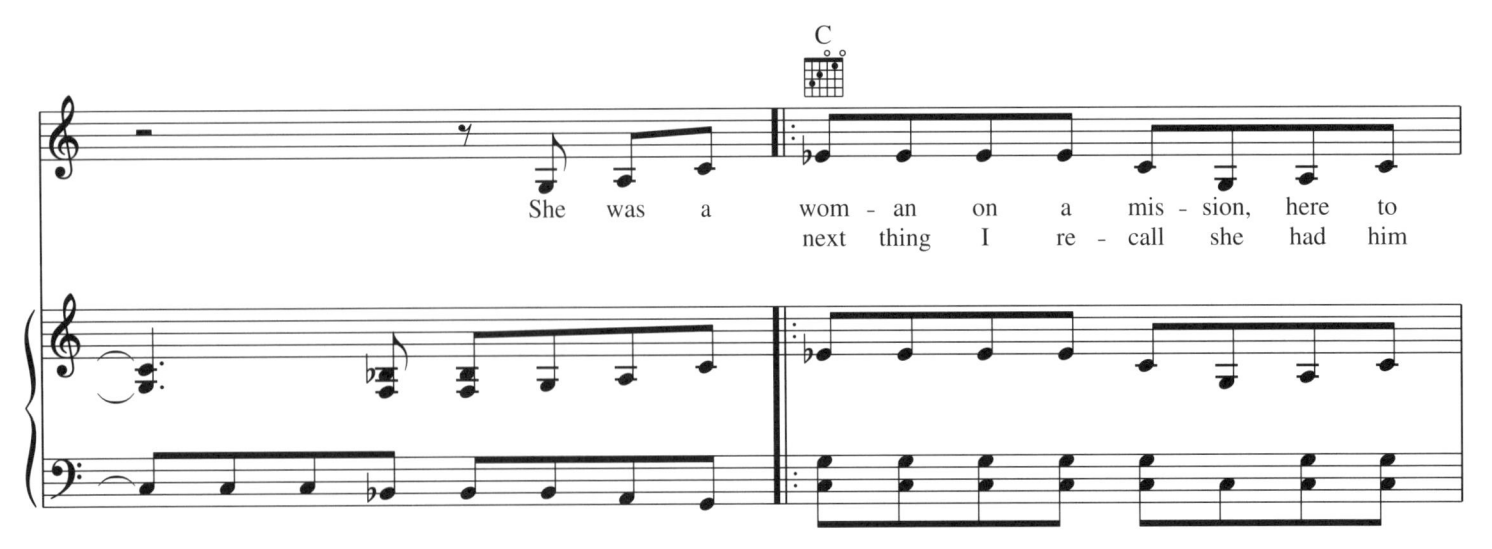

Lyrics:
She was a wom-an on a mis-sion, here to
next thing I re-call she had him

Original key: B major. This edition has been transposed up one half-step to be more playable.

Copyright © 2000 by Acuff-Rose Music, Inc., Thea Later Music, Curb Songs, Charlie Monk Music and Mick Hits
All Rights Reserved   Used by Permission

drown him and for-get him. So I set her up ___ a-gain to wash him
back a-gainst the wall, chew-in' him like a bull-dog on a

down. She had just a-bout suc-ceed-ed when that
bone. She was put-tin' him in his place and I mean

low-down, no-good, cheat-in', good for noth-in' came strut-tin' through the
right up in his face, drag-gin' him down a list of done-me-

crowd. Oh, he was lay-in' it on ___ so thick, he
wrongs. Oh, it was just __ a-bout __ now ___ that the crowd _

never missed a lick, pro-fess-ing his nev-er end-ing
_____ gath-ered 'round. They'd come to watch him pay for his ev-'ry

love. Oh, but I nev-er will _____ for-get when
sin. She called him ev-'ry-thing un-der the sun and when we

she stood up and said, *(Spoken:)* "So I guess you think we're just gonna kiss and make up, don't you?" That's when she said,
thought that she was done, *(Spoken:)* she reared back and let him have it again, man. She said, she said,

"Why don't you kiss, kiss

this? And I don't mean on my ros-y red lips. Me and you ah we're through and there's on-ly one thing left for you to do. You just come on o-ver here one last time. Puck-er up and close your eyes and kiss this good-bye."

Well, the this. Hey, kiss this. And I don't mean on my ros-y red lips. Me and you, ah, we're through and there's on-ly one thing left for you to do. You just come on o-ver here one last time. Puck-er up and close your eyes and kiss this good-bye. Hey, kiss this good-bye." *Spoken: See ya.*

A LITTLE GASOLINE

Words and Music by TAMMY ROGERS and DEAN MILLER

Moderately

Throw-in' pic-tures out the win-dow, scat-tered by the way the wind blows.
talked in cir-cles till the words ran out and it all came down to an an-gry shout. Be-

Bye bye, ba-by, that's the last I'll see of you.
fore I knew it, I was in third gear and gone. So

Copyright © 1998, 2000 Sony/ATV Tunes LLC and Mighty Nice Music (BMI)
All Rights on behalf of Sony/ATV Tunes LLC Administered by Sony/ATV Music Publishing, 8 Music Square West, Nashville, TN 37203
All Rights on behalf of Mighty Nice Music Administered by Bluewater Music Corp.
International Copyright Secured   All Rights Reserved

Shoe box full of old love letters, I'll tear each one till I
this had been comin' for a long long time. If I said I'm sorry, well I'd

feel better and I won't look back, 'cause I don't like the view.
be lyin'. If you think I'll never make it, well you'd be wrong.

And what my heart needs

now is rest, so I'm packin' up and I'm headed west. My

mind's made up, ___ I'll put it to the test. ___

Push-ing my-self and this old ma-chine, ___ burn-in' fumes ___ and what's

left of my dreams. Let 'em go, _____ 'cause I don't need ___ no

strings. Just give me a road ___ and a

lit - tle gas - o - line.

We

What my heart needs now is rest, so I'm packin' up and I'm headed west. My mind's made up, I'll put it to the test. Pushing myself and this old machine, burnin' fumes and what's left of my dreams. Let 'em go, 'cause

I don't need no strings. Just give me a road and a little gas-o-line. Just give me a road and a little gas-o-line.

LOVE'S THE ONLY HOUSE

Words and Music by TOM DOUGLAS
and BUZZ CASON

Moderately

I was standin' in the groc-'ry store line, the one they marked ex - press, when this wom-an came through with a-bout twen-ty-five things. And I said, "Don't you know that more is less?" She said, "This

Copyright © 1999 Sony/ATV Songs LLC, Buzz Cason Publications and Southern Writers Group
All Rights on behalf of Sony/ATV Songs LLC Administered by Sony/ATV Music Publishing, 8 Music Square West, Nashville, TN 37203
International Copyright Secured   All Rights Reserved

world is mov-in' so fast ___ I just get ___ more be-hind ___ ev-'ry-day. and ev-'ry morn-in' when I make my cof-fee, I can't be-lieve my life's turned out this way." All I could say was, "Love's ___ the on-ly house big ___ e-nough for all the pain ___ in the world. ___

Love's the on-ly house big e-nough for all the pain."

He was walk-in' by the oth-er day and I said, "Hey ba-by, how you been?" Yeah, I got me a lit-tle girl now and she's four years old and she's got her dad-dy's lit-tle grin.

You on-ly want-ed what you can't have and, ba-by, you can't have me now.

I gave my heart to an-oth-er, yeah, I'm a moth-er and he's a fa-ther and we're a fam-'ly and we got each oth-er and I found out the hard way that love's the on-ly house big e-nough for all the pain in the world.

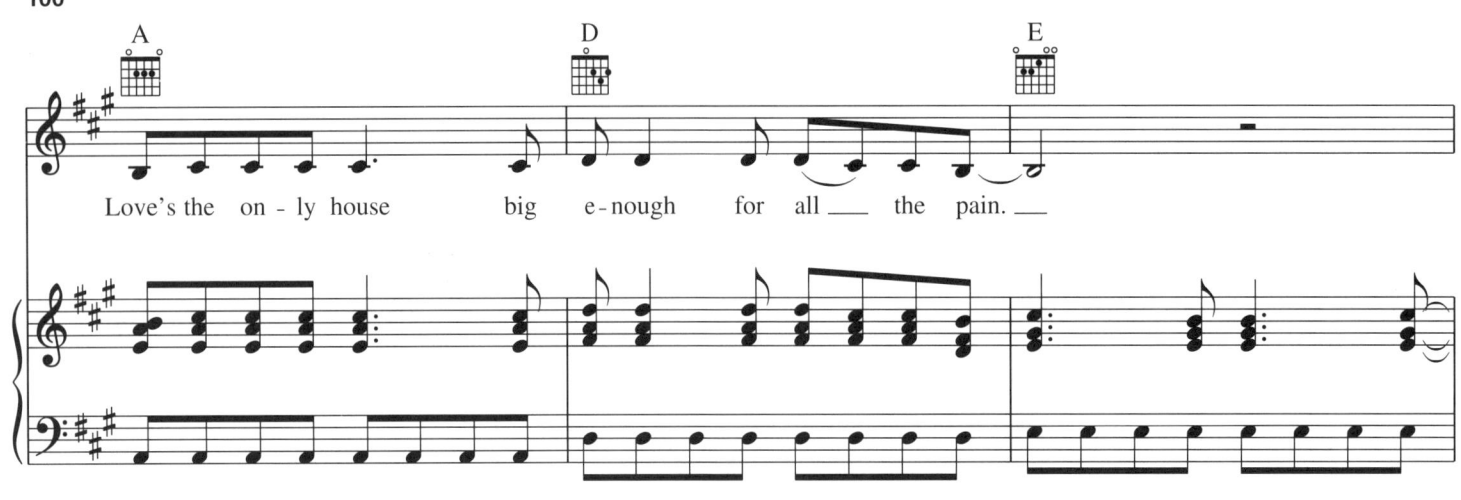

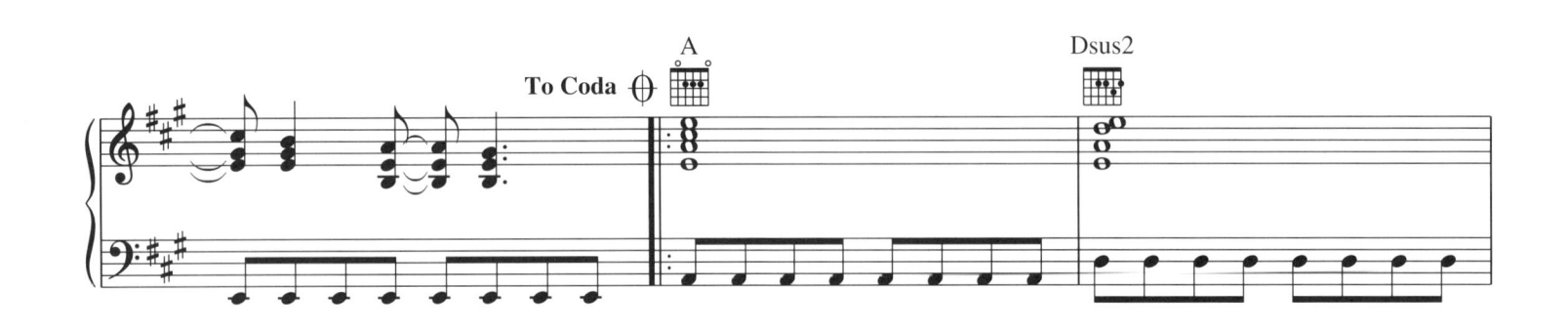

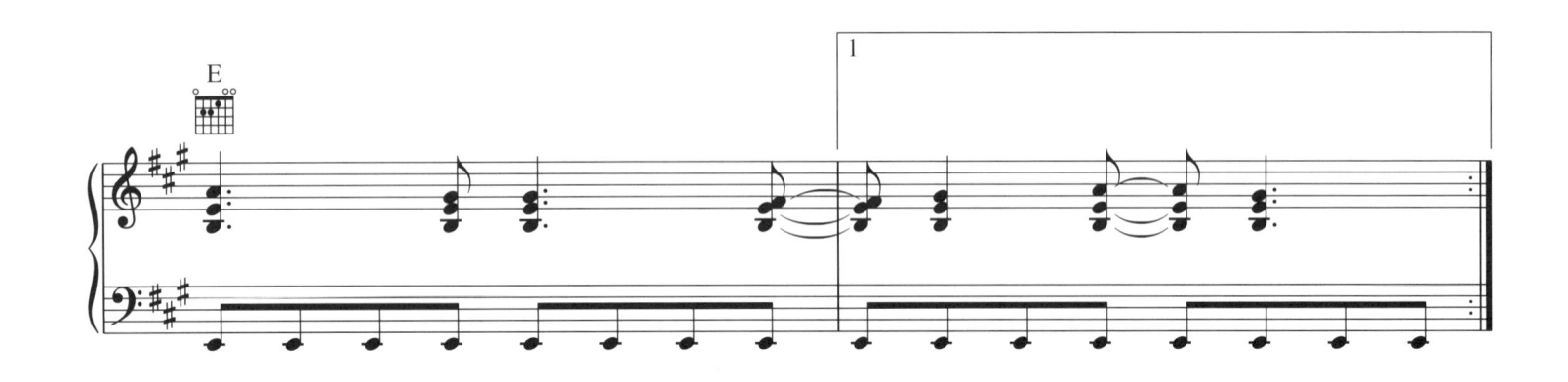

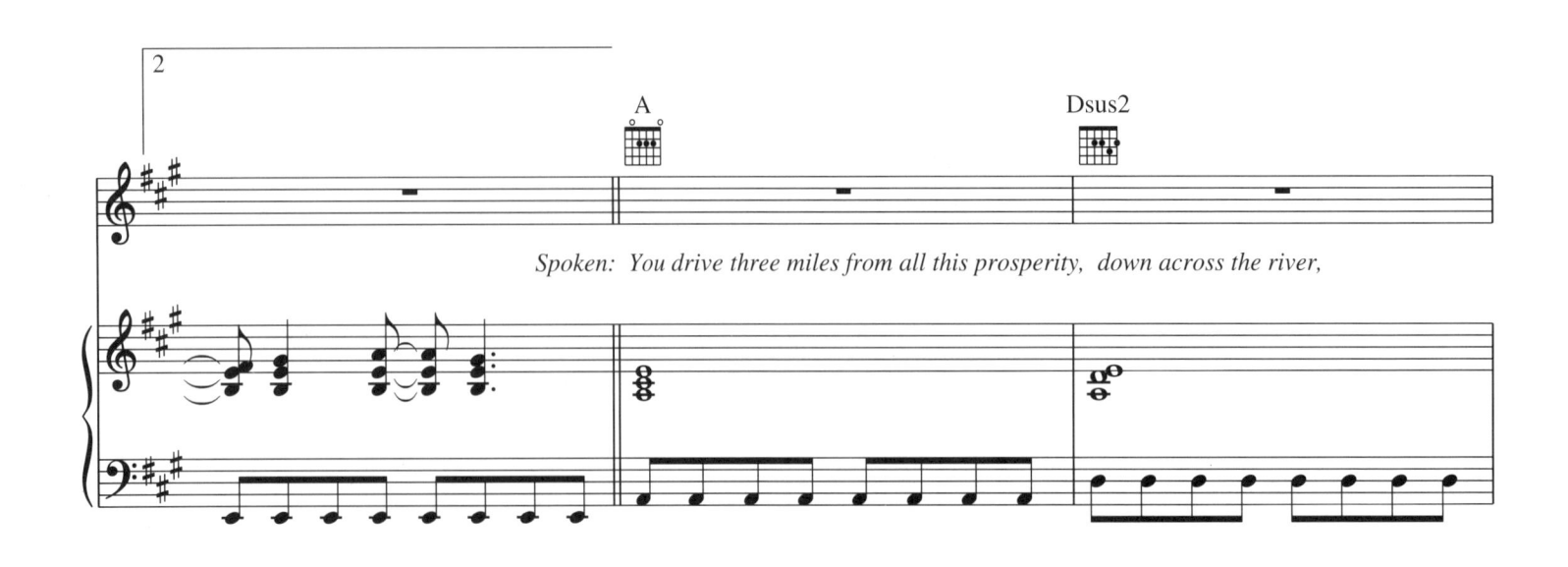

Love's the on-ly house big e-nough for all the pain.

Spoken: You drive three miles from all this prosperity, down across the river,

and you see a ghetto there.   *And we got children walkin' around with guns and they got knives and drugs and pain to spare.*

And here I am in my clean, white shirt with a lit-tle mon-ey in my pock-et and a nice warm home. And we got teen-ag-ers walk-

-in' a-round in a cul-ture of dark-ness, liv-in' to-geth-er a-lone. All I can say is love's

CODA

And I can't ex-plain it and I can't un-der-stand. But I've come down to get my hands dirt-y and to-geth-er we'll make a stand.

Some-where 'cross the park-in' lot some band's play-in' out of tune. Cit-y streets are gon-na burn if we don't do some-thin' soon. A se-ñor-i-ta can't quit cry'n', ba-by's due now an-y day. Don Juan left, got sick of try'n', no one there to show him the way. *Spoken: She came down to the grocery store. She said, "I, I wanna buy a little carton of milk, but I don't have any money."*

I said, "Hey, I'll cover you, honey, 'cause the pain's gotta go somewhere. Yeah, the pain has gotta go some place. So, come on down to my house."

Don't you know that

Love's the on-ly house big e-nough for all the pain in the world.

Love's the on-ly house big e-nough for all the pain.

Don't you know that love's the on-ly house big

e-nough for all of the pain in the world.

Love's the on-ly house big e-nough for all the pain, yeah.

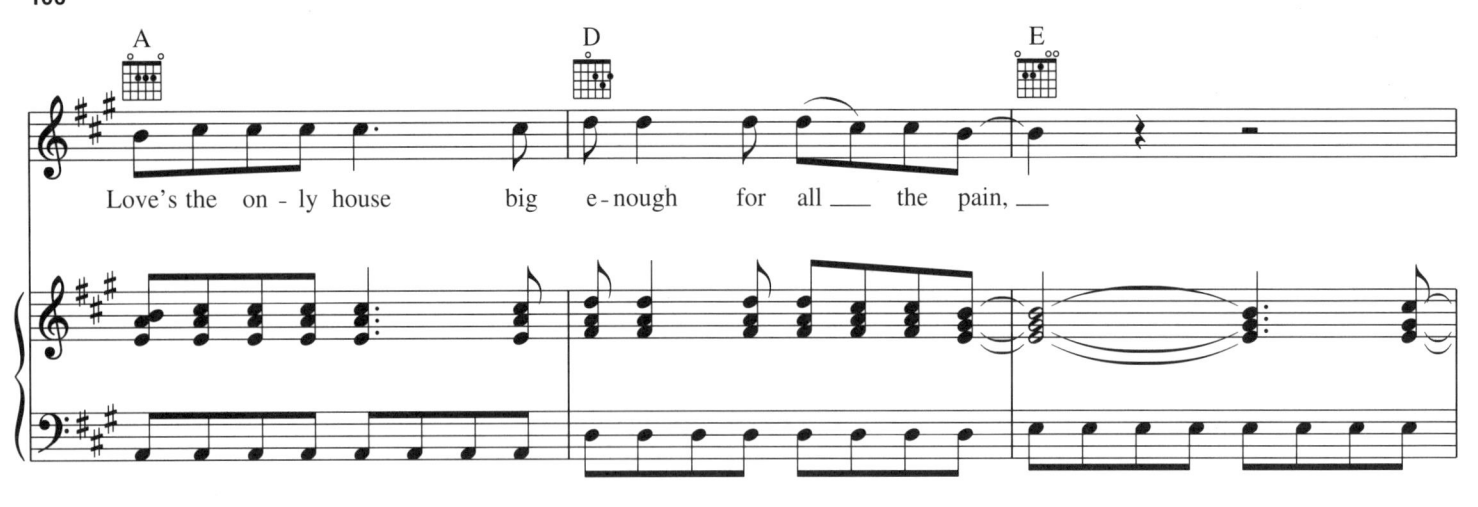

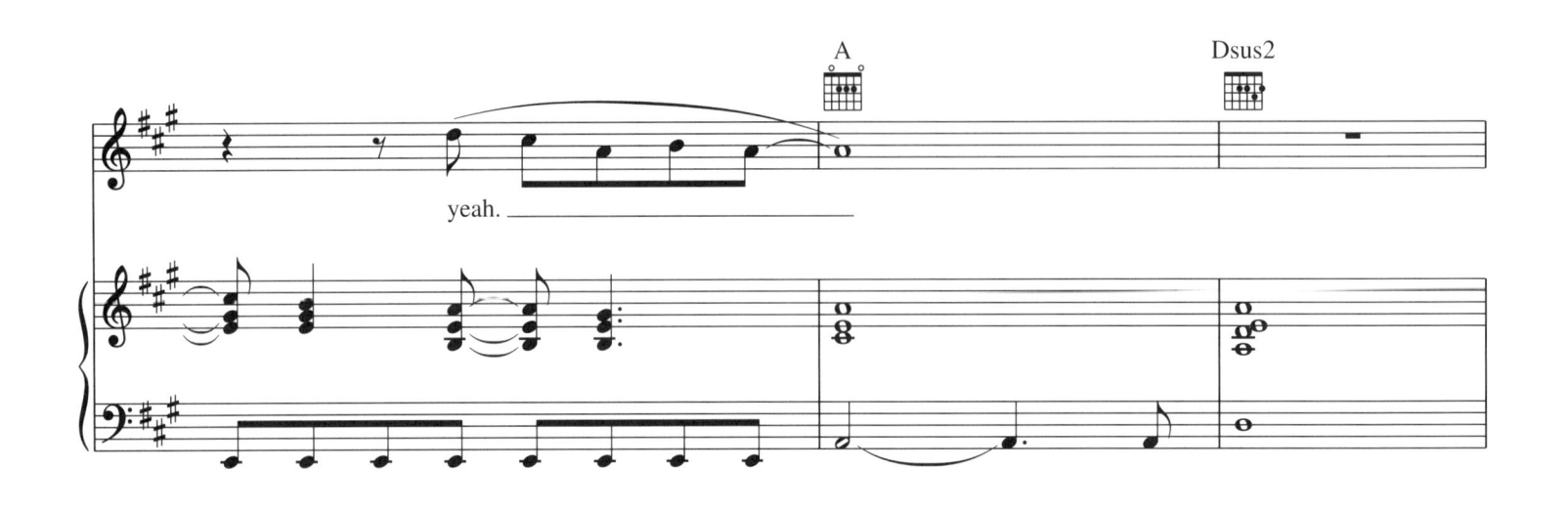

Repeat and Fade

Opt. Ending

WE DANCED

Words and Music by BRAD PAISLEY
and CHRIS DuBOIS

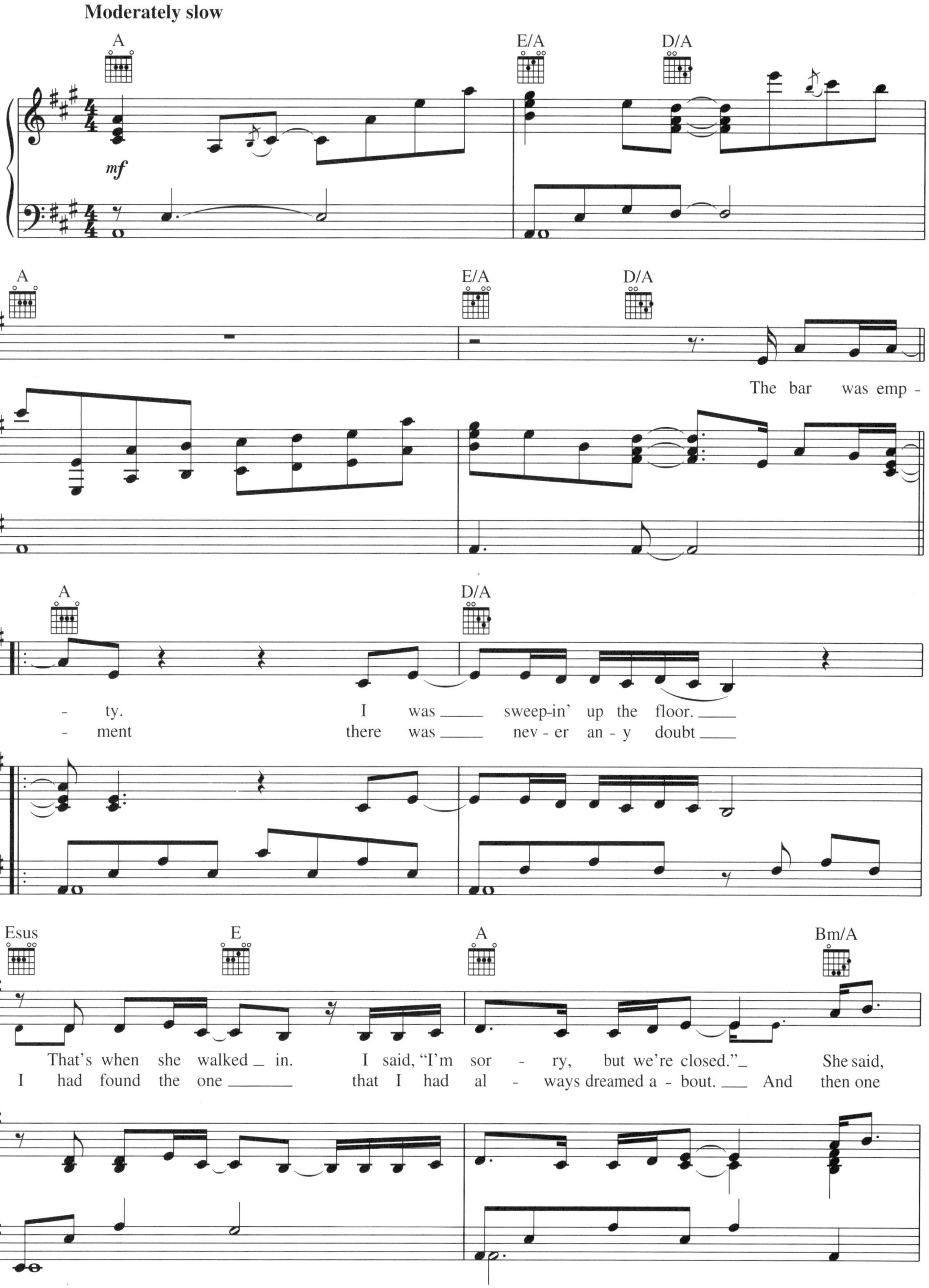

"I know, but I'm a-fraid I left my purse." I said, "I
eve-nin' when she stopped by af-ter work, I

put one back be-hind the bar. I bet it's prob-'ly yours." And the
pulled a dia-mond ring out of the pock-et of my shirt. And as her

next thing that I knew, there we were lost in con-ver-
eyes filled up with tears, she said, "This is the last thing I ex-pect-

sa-tion. Be-fore I
-ed." And then she

handed her her purse, I said, "You'll only get this back on one con-
took me by the hand and said, "I'll only marry you on one con-
di - tion."
di - tion." And we danced
out there on that emp - ty hard - wood floor. The
chairs up and the lights turned way down low. The

music played, we held each other close and we danced. And from that mo- and we danced like no one else had ever danced before. I can't ex-plain what hap-pened on that floor, but the music played, we held each other close and we danced. Yeah, we danced.

MY BEST FRIEND

Words and Music by AIMEE MAYO
and BILL LUTHER

I nev-er had no one that I could count on.
You stand by me and you be-lieve in me

I've been let down so man-y times.
like no-bod-y ev-er has.

Copyright © 1999 by Careers-BMG Music Publishing, Inc.
International Copyright Secured   All Rights Reserved

And I was tired of hurtin', so tired of search-in' till you walked in to my life. It was a feel-in' I'd nev-er known. And for the first

When my world goes cra-zy, you're right there to save me. You make me see how much I have. And I still trem-ble when we touch. And, oh, the look

_____ time _____ I didn't feel alone. You're more _____
in your eyes _____ when we make love.

_____ than a lover. There could never be an-

other to make me feel the way _____ you do.

Oh, _____ we just get closer. I fall in love all o-

-ver ev-'ry time I look at you.

I don't know where I'd be without you here with me.

Life with you makes perfect sense. You're my best

friend. You're my best friend,

D
A/C♯
oh, yeah.
2
E/G♯
Em/G
D/F♯
friend.
Ooh, oh, ooh, oh.
You're my best friend,
D
A/C♯
E
D.S. al Coda
uh, huh.
You're
cresc.
CODA
A
N.C.
E/G♯
Bm7
2 fr
friend.
Oh, whoa, ooh, oh.

117

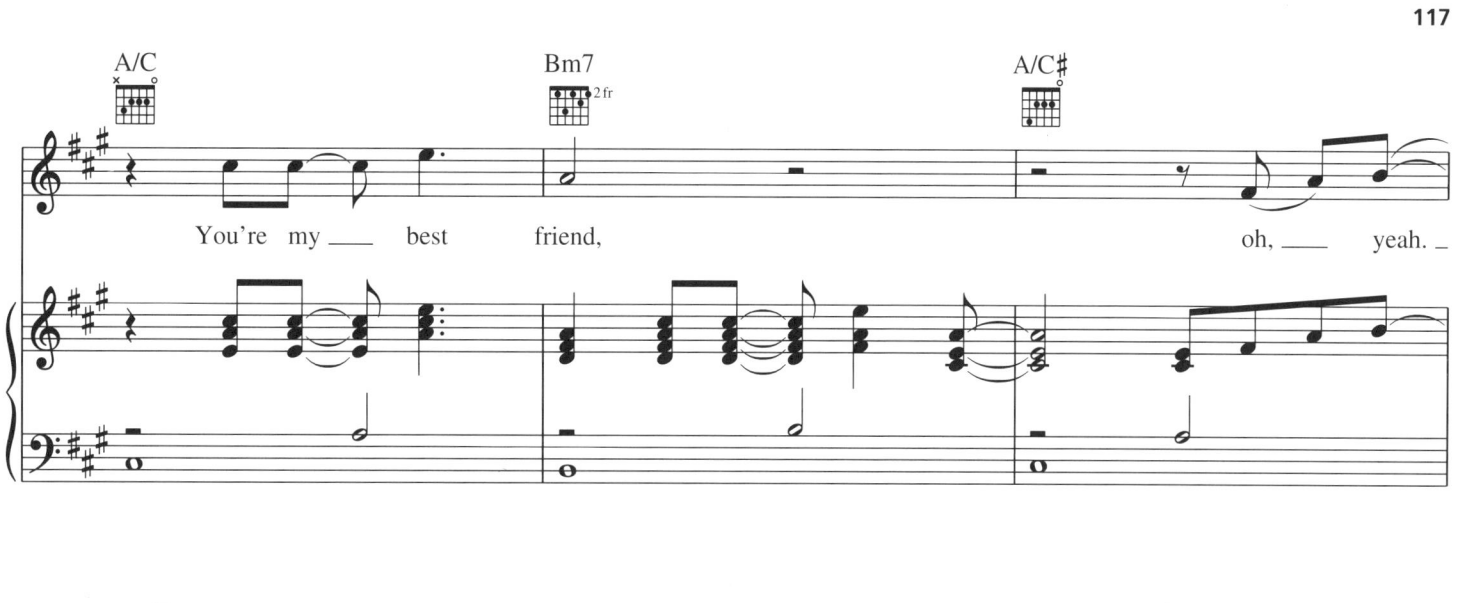

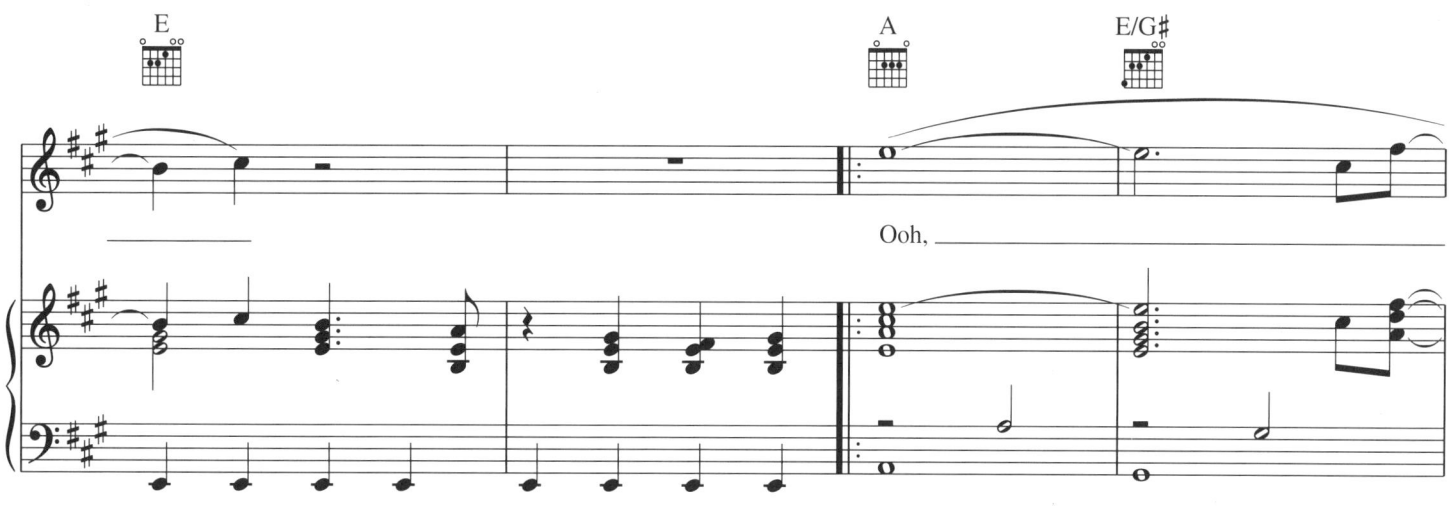

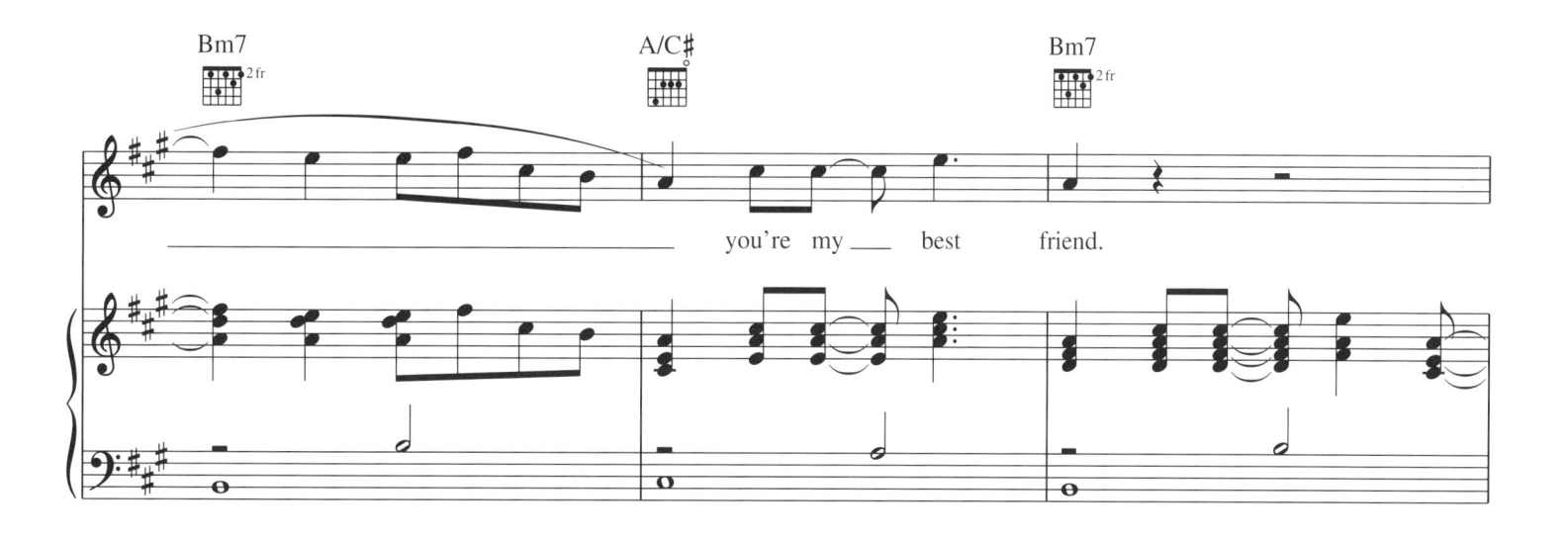

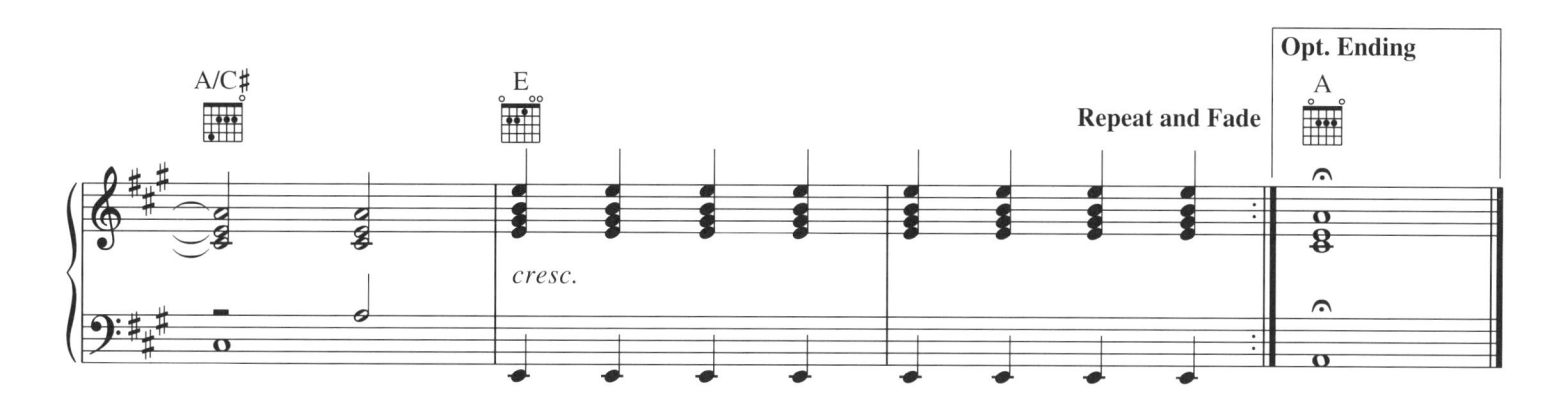

MY NEXT THIRTY YEARS

Words and Music by
PHIL VASSAR

Moderately

think I'll take a moment, celebrate my age, the ending of an era and the turning of a page. Now it's time to focus in on where I go from here. Lord, have mercy on my next thirty years.

In my next thir-ty years _ I'm gon-na have some fun, try to for-get a-bout _ all the craz-y things _ I've done. May-be now I've con-quered all _ my

| C | A/C# | Dm | B♭ | F | C |

ad - o - les - cent fears and I'll do it bet - ter in __ my

| B♭ | F | Dm | C |

next thir - ty years. My next thir - ty years I'm gon - na
next thir - ty years will be the

| B♭ | F/A | B♭ | F/A |

set - tle all __ the scores, __ cry a lit - tle less, __
best years of __ my life. __ Raise a lit - tle __ fam - i - ly __ and

| C | A/C# | Dm | C |

laugh a lit - tle more, find a world of hap - pi - ness __ with -
hang out with my wife. Spend __ pre - cious mo - ments with __ the

Bb F/A Bb F/A
out the hate and fear, fig - ure out just what I'm do - in' here
ones that I hold dear. Make up for lost time here
Gm7 Bb/C F C7sus/F
To Coda
in my next thir - ty years.
in my next thir - ty
F C7sus/F Dm C
Instrumental solo
Bb F/A Bb F/A

Solo ends Oh my next thir-ty years ___

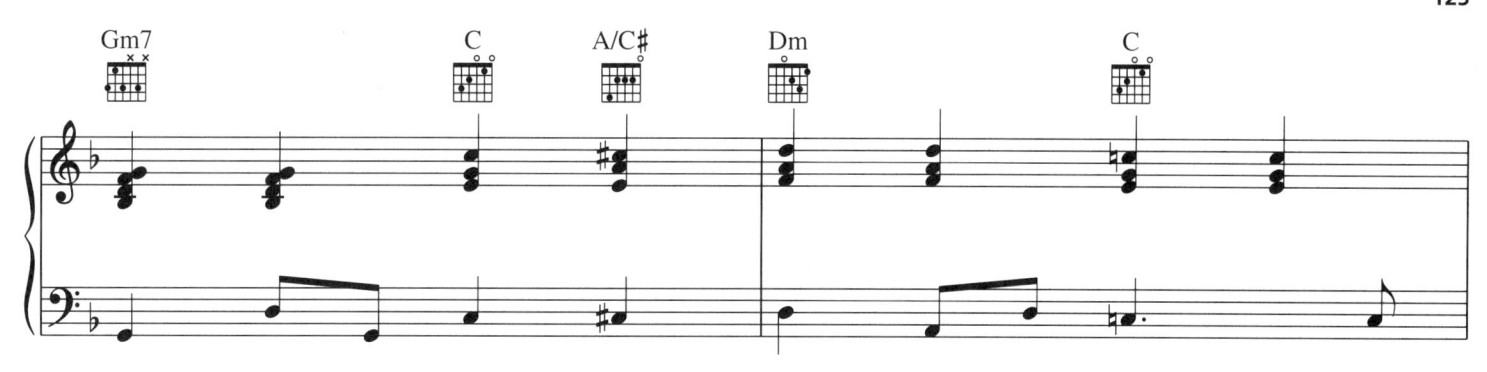

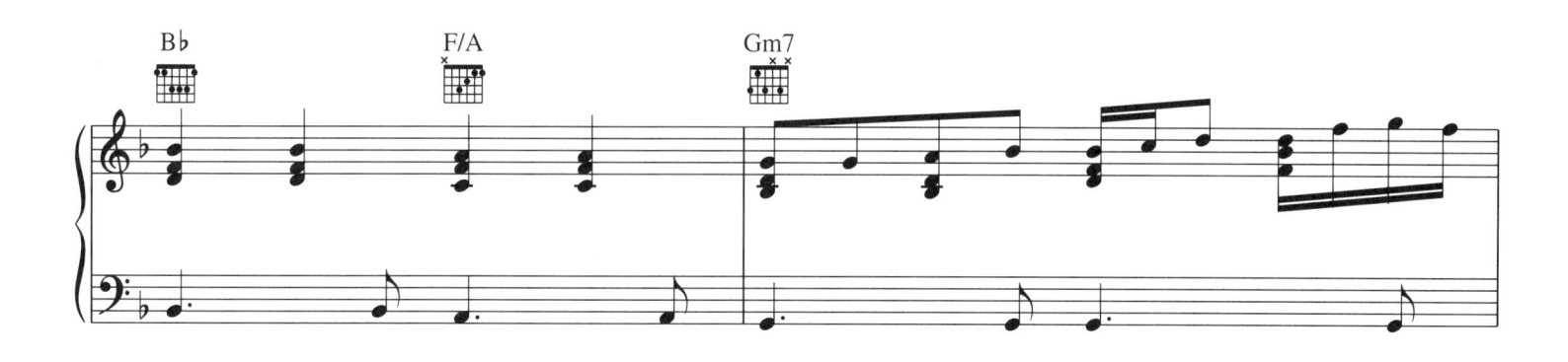

I'm gon-na watch my weight, eat a few more sal-ads and

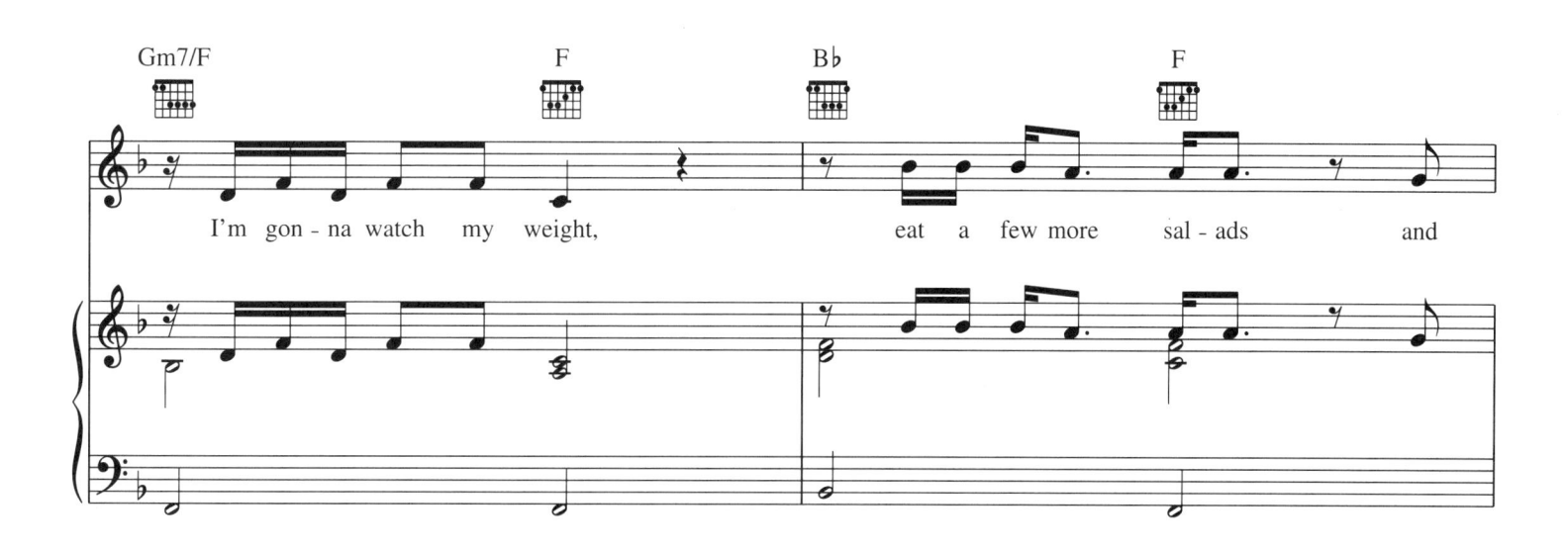

not stay up __ so late. Drink a lit-tle lem-on-ade __ and

not so man-y beers. May-be I'll re-mem-ber my next thir-ty years.

D.S. al Coda

My

CODA

years,

in my

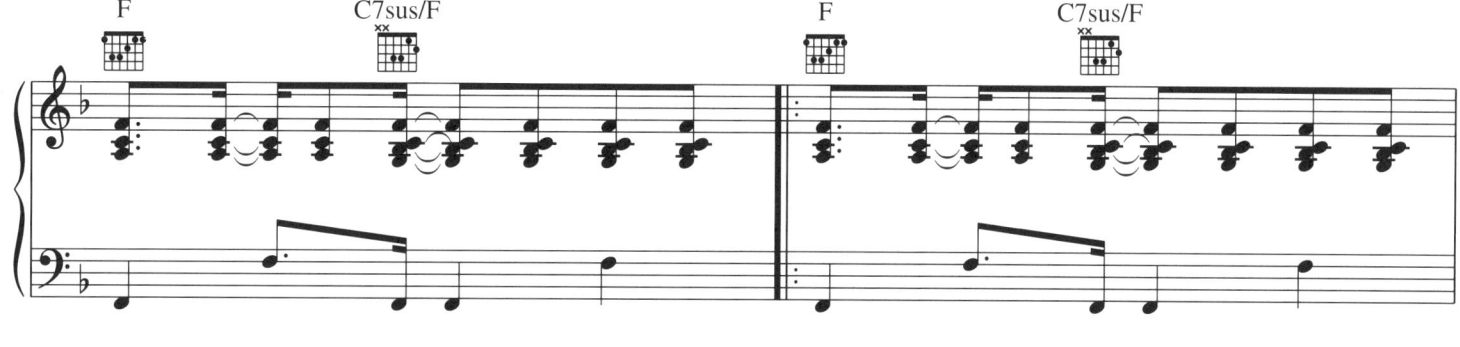

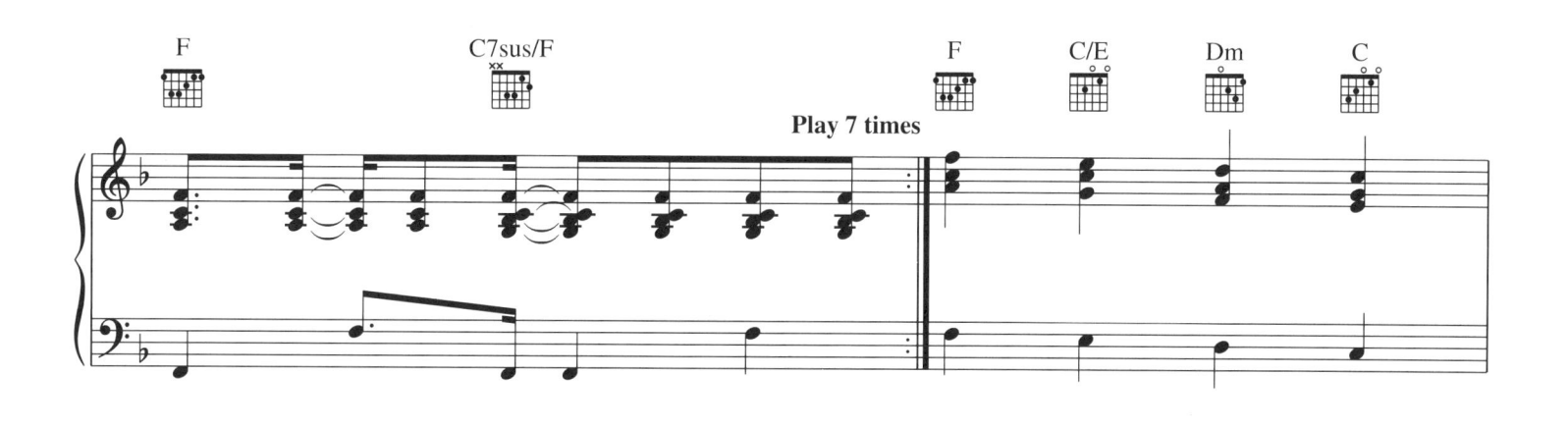

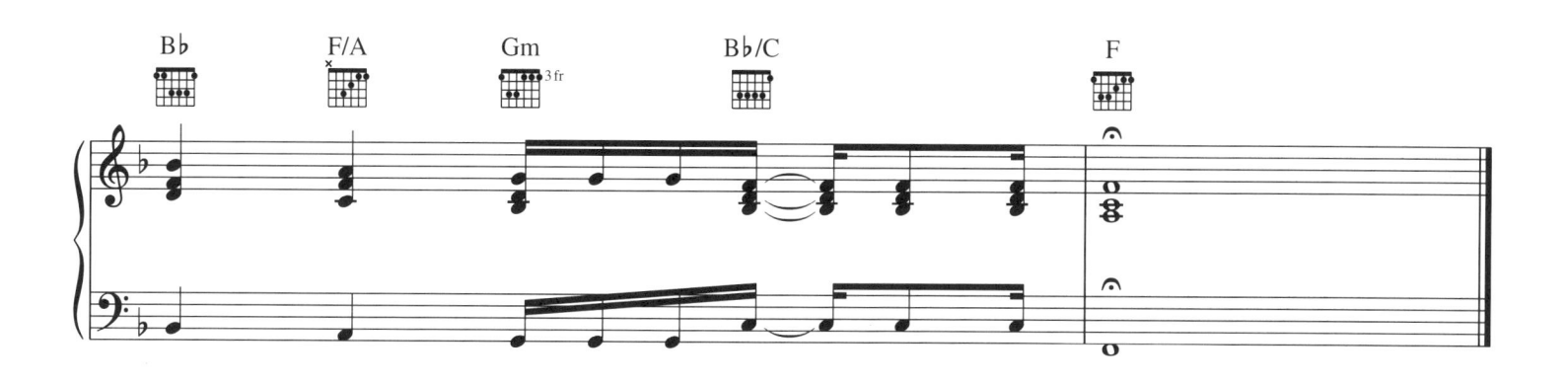

next thir - ty years.

ONE VOICE

Words and Music by DON COOK
and DAVID MALLOY

Moderately slow

Some kids have and some kids don't, and some of us are won-der-ing why.
house, a yard, a neigh-bor-hood where you could ride your new bike to school.

And Mom won't watch the news at night; there's too much stuff that's mak-ing her cry.
A kind-a world where Mom and Dad still be-lieve the gold-en rule.

We need some help
Life's not that sim - ple
(D.S.) Thanks for the help

Copyright © 2000 Sony/ATV Songs LLC, Don Cook Music, Starstruck Angel Music, Inc. and Malloy's Toys Music
All Rights on behalf of Sony/ATV Songs LLC and Don Cook Music Administered by Sony/ATV Music Publishing, 8 Music Square West, Nashville, TN 37203
International Copyright Secured   All Rights Reserved

down here on earth.
down here on earth.
down here on earth.

A thousand prayers, a million words, but one voice was heard.

One voice, one simple word.

Hearts know what to say. One dream can change the world. Keep believin' till you find your way.

Yesterday while walkin' home, I saw some kid on Newbury Road.

He pulled a pis-tol from his bag and tossed it in the riv-er be-low.

D.S. al Coda (take 2nd ending)

CODA

One voice was heard. One voice was heard.

rit.

THE WAY YOU LOVE ME

Words and Music by MICHAEL DULANEY
and KEITH FOLLESE

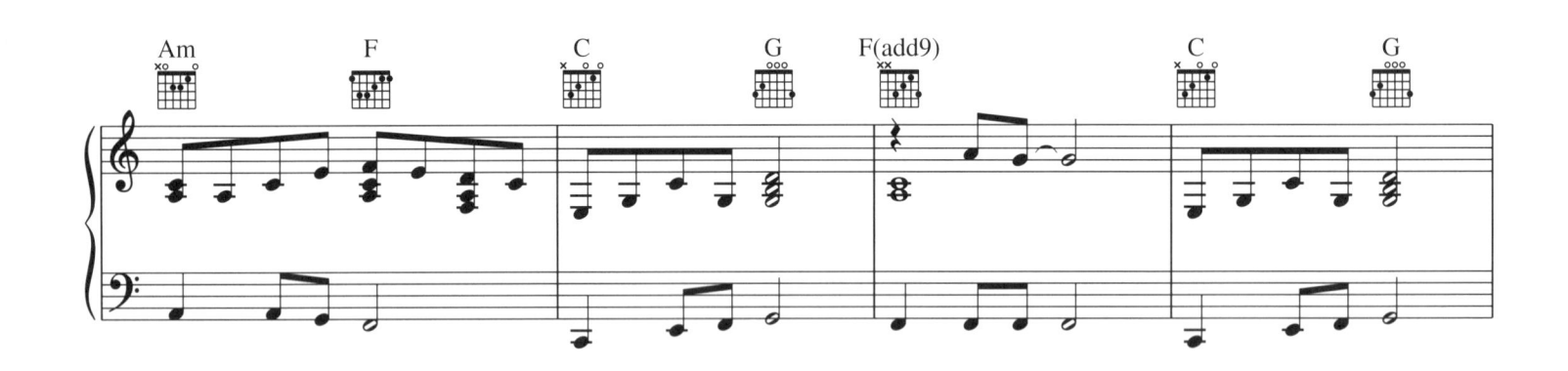

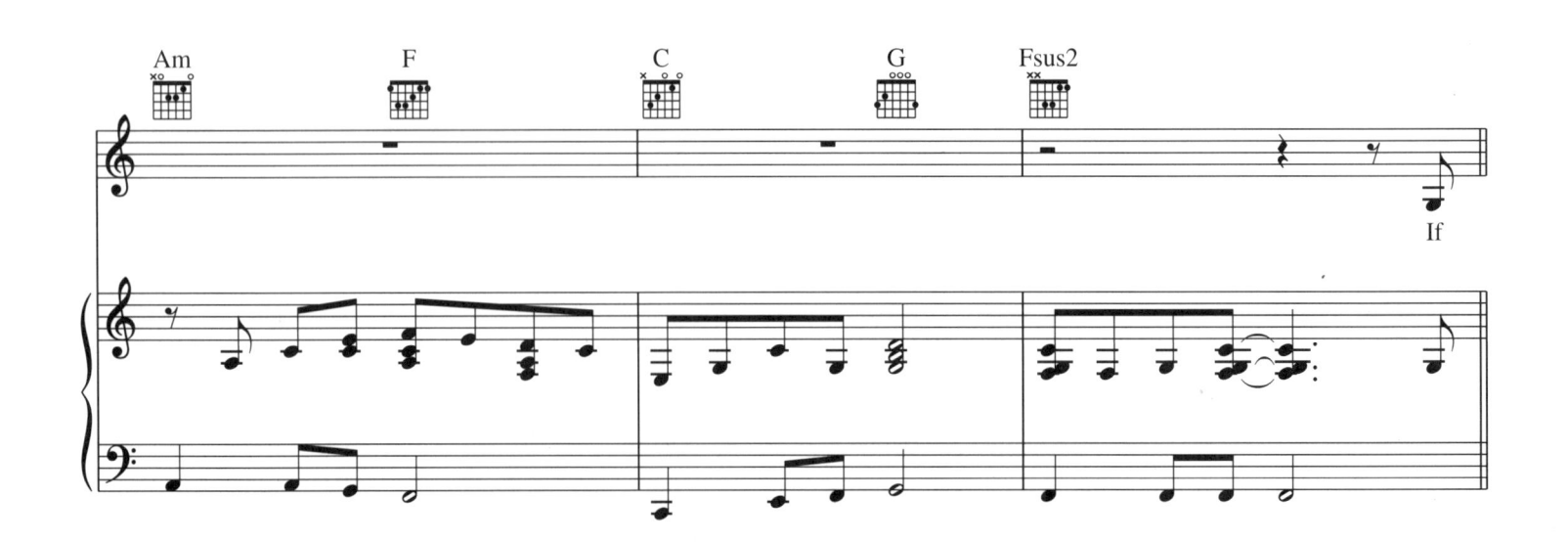

Moderately bright beat

If

C G F G C G
I could grant you one wish, I wish you could see the
It's not right. It's not fair. What you're miss - ing
F G C B♭ F G
way you kiss. Ooh, I love watch - ing you, ba - by,
o - ver there. Some - day I'll find a way to show you
C B♭ F G A D A
when you're driv - ing me, ooh, cra - zy.
just how luck - y I am to know you.
Ooh, I love the way you,
G A D A Em D/F♯ G A
love the way you love me. There's no - where else I'd rath - er be.
(When you touch me)
(drives me wild.)

D A G A Em D/F♯ G
Ooh, to feel the way I feel with your arms a - round me. I on - ly wish that you could
A B E B C♯m A
To Coda
see the way you love me. Whoa oh oh, the way you
(love me)
1
E B A
love me.
2
E B C♯m7
love me.
A B G
You're the mil - lion rea - sons why there's love re - flect - ing

133

WITHOUT YOU

Words and Music by NATALIE MAINES
and ERIC SILVER

Moderately

I've sure en-joyed ____ the rain, ____ but I'm
Nev-er thought ____ I'd be ____ lying

look-in' for-ward to ____ the sun. ____ You have to feel ____ the pain
here with-out ____ you by ____ my side. ____ It seems un-real ____ to me

when you lose the love ____ you gave ____ some-one. I
that the life you prom-ised was ____ a lie. ____ You

© 1999 SCRAPIN' TOAST MUSIC (ASCAP)/Administered by BUG MUSIC, EMI APRIL MUSIC INC. and 703 MUSIC
All Rights for 703 MUSIC Controlled and Administered by EMI APRIL MUSIC INC.
All Rights Reserved   Used by Permission

135

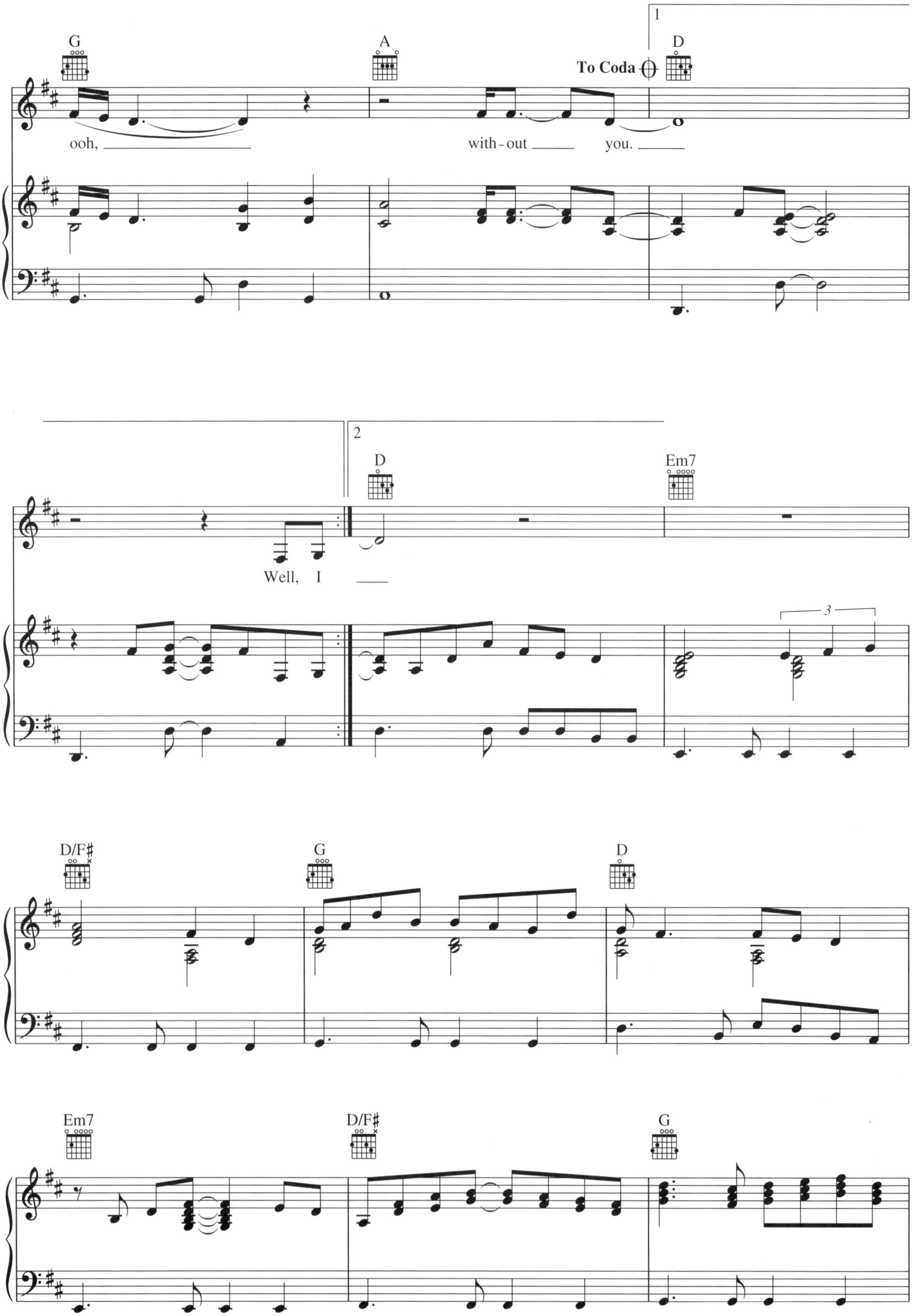
G
A
1
To Coda
D
ooh,
with - out
you.
2
D
Em7
Well, I
3
D/F♯
G
D
Em7
D/F♯
G

Some-bod-y tell my head ___ to try to tell my heart ___ that I'm bet-ter off with-out ___ you. 'Cause, ba-by, I can't live. ___ With-out you ___ I'm not ___

CODA

With-out ___ you. ___

WHAT ABOUT NOW

Words and Music by RON HARBIN,
ANTHONY SMITH and AARON BARKER

Moderately fast

... in the win-dow said for sale or trade on the last re-main-ing din-o-saur

Copyright © 2000 Sony/ATV Tunes LLC, Ron Harbin Music, O-Tex Music, Blind Sparrow Music, WB Music Corp. and Notes To Music
All Rights on behalf of Ron Harbin Music Administered by
Sony/ATV Music Publishing, 8 Music Square West, Nashville, TN 37203
All Rights on behalf of Blind Sparrow Music Administered by O-Tex Music
International Copyright Secured   All Rights Reserved

Detroit made. Seven hundred dollars was a heck of a deal for a four-hundred horse power juke box on wheels. And that road rolls out like a welcome mat. I don't know where it goes, but it beats where we're at. We always said someday somehow we're gonna

-tin' this off, baby, long enough. Just give me the word and we'll be kickin' up dust. We both know it's just a matter of time till our

get a-way,_ gon-na blow_ this town._
hearts start rac - in' for that coun-ty line._

What a-bout now?_ How 'bout to-night?_ Ba-by, for once_ let's don't_ think_ twice._

Let's take_ that spin_ that nev - er ends_ that_ we've_ been talk - in' a-bout._ What a-bout now?_ Why should we wait?_

We can chase these dreams down the interstate and be long gone 'fore the world moves on and makes another round.

What about now?

We've been put — What about now?

We could hang a-round this town for-ev-er makin' plans, but there won't ev-er be a bet-ter time to take this chance. What a-bout now? How 'bout to-night?

Ba-by, for once let's don't think twice. Let's take that spin that never ends that we've been talkin' about. What about now? Why should we wait? We can chase these dreams down the interstate and be long gone 'fore the world

144